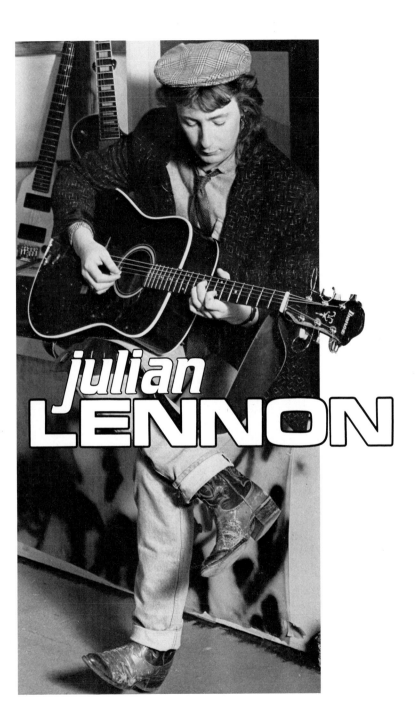

julian LENNON

Seymour

by D. L. Mabery

Lerner Publications Company
Minneapolis

Photo Credits:
Scott Weiner/Retna Ltd., pp. 1, 6, 26, 32; UPI/Bettmann Newsphotos,
pp. 10, 14, 39; Richard Young/Retna Ltd., 18, 28, 30; Ron Wolfson/
Photofeatures, p. 21; Kevin Mazur/Retna Ltd., p. 34; Phyllis Rosney/
Starfile Photo Agency, pp. 2, 36

Front cover photo by Richard Aaron/Starfile Photo Agency
Back cover photo by Pictorial Press/Starfile Photo Agency

Manufactured in the United States of America

LIBRARY OF CONGRESS CATALOGING-IN-PUBLICATION DATA

Mabery, D. L.
  Julian Lennon.

  Summary: A biography of the first son of John
Lennon, a member of the Beatles, now a recording star
himself.
    1. Lennon, Julian, 1963-   . 2. Rock musicians—
England—Biography—Juvenile literature. [1. Lennon,
Julian, 1963-   . 2. Musicians] I. Title.
ML3930.L35M3 1986 784.5′4′00924 [B] [92] 85-24009
ISBN 0-8225-1607-1 (lib. bdg.)

1 2 3 4 5 6 7 8 9 10 94 93 92 91 90 89 88 87 86

Contents

Rock Legend's Son

Even before Julian Lennon recorded his first album, *Valotte*, at the age of 21, he'd already had such a profound influence on the course of rock 'n' roll music that his name would have gone into the history books. Without knowing it, Julian managed to inspire the Beatles — the most famous and influential rock group in the history of popular music — to write and record two songs. One of those songs became the group's biggest selling single.

Julian today, a serious musician. Behind him on the bulletin board is a copy of the *Rolling Stone* cover which featured the Beatles.

Julian is, of course, the first son of John Lennon, a member of the Beatles.

With John Lennon on vocals and rhythm guitar, Paul McCartney on vocals and bass, George Harrison on lead guitar and vocals, and Ringo Starr on drums, the Beatles burst upon the music scene in the early 1960s. The group saw their albums rise immediately to Number One on the charts, the Beatles' songs could be heard everywhere: on the radio, on television, and in the movies. The Beatles became so popular and well-liked that they inspired a number of other musicians to follow in their footsteps. A number of musicians who became stars in the late 1970s and early 1980s have said that they were inspired by the Beatles to begin writing and performing songs.

Julian Lennon was born at the time his father was just becoming a big star. He grew up during the years his father was touring and recording music for the Beatles. While the Beatles were in the recording studio working on their masterpiece album, *Sgt. Pepper's Lonely Hearts Club Band*, Julian was in London area grade school.

One day young Julian brought home a drawing he had done of a girl in school named Lucy. Julian showed the drawing to his father. It was of a girl with blond hair surrounded by stars. When John asked what the drawing was, Julian proudly informed his dad that the artwork was "Lucy in the sky!"

John Lennon liked his son's image so much, he began writing a song about Lucy in the sky. The elder Lennon titled his song "Lucy in the Sky with Diamonds," and the Beatles recorded the song for the *Sgt. Pepper's* album.

When it was released in 1967, *Sgt. Pepper's Lonely Hearts Club Band* topped anything that the Beatles or anyone else had ever done. Every song on the album sounded remarkable and new. That particular Beatles album changed the course of rock music forever by ushering in new recording techniques, using symphony orchestras, and singing songs with more "grown up" lyrics than were normally heard in rock songs. And Julian Lennon was a part of that process.

Julian's other historical contribution to rock music happened the next year. In 1968 John divorced Julian's mother, Cynthia, so he could marry Yoko Ono, the woman he would live with until his death in 1980. Paul McCartney, who had spent a lot of time playing with young Julian, wrote a little song to cheer up the five-year-old boy. On the way over to visit Julian one day, Paul thought, "Hey Julian, it's not so bad. Take a sad song and make it better." Paul began working the line around, and the idea eventually became the hit single "Hey Jude," a song which became the Beatles' most successful single ever.

With a history such as his, it might seem logical that young Julian Lennon would become a recording artist. Yet, the road from being the son of a popular rock star to becoming a rock star in his own right was a long and winding one. Julian had to overcome the special problems of being the son of a famous person — to get people to recognize him for his own talents, and not for who his father was.

The Legend Begins

John Lennon married Cynthia Powell in the late summer of 1962, before the Beatles had a recording contract and before the string of hit singles began. By January of 1963, a single titled "Please Please Me" was released in England, and the Beatles became the latest rage with the kids. In March the group recorded its first album,

John Lennon with his first wife, Cynthia — Julian's mother. During their marriage, Cynthia put up with screaming teenaged girls who followed the Beatles everywhere, business managers who didn't want it known that any of the Beatles was married, and reporters and photographers chasing John for a good story or picture.

11

and it quickly rose to the top of the British charts. Because of the hit single and album, John was away on tour when his first son, John Charles Julian Lennon, was born on April 8, 1963. It was a week after his son's birth that John managed to visit the hospital where his wife and child were.

Getting into the hospital to visit his wife and son wasn't easy for John Lennon. Because of the new-found fame that now surrounded him, John was forced to disguise himself with a false mustache and dark glasses as he dashed through the hallways of the Sefton General Hospital in Liverpool to see his son. When he saw Julian, John picked him up, cradled him in his arm, and said, "Now, who's going to be a famous little rocker like his dad?"

Before too long, someone recognized John Lennon in the hospital, and a small crowd began to gather outside the room. John decided he'd better leave before he attracted too much attention.

With each new record, the popularity of the Beatles increased. John Lennon was forever away on a tour or in the recording studio and had less and less time to spend with his son. In fact, for the first six months of his son's life John hardly saw Julian at all. Because John Lennon and the Beatles were so popular with teenaged girls, the managers of the rock group did not want it to become known that one of the Beatles was married and had a child. So Julian and Cynthia had to be kept a secret from the rest of the world, and for a while they lived in total secrecy in the house of John's aunt, Mimi.

Eventually the news did get out that John Lennon was married, and by the end of 1963 the world got its first look at Julian Lennon. As it turned out, Julian grew up surrounded by attention.

Somebody
to Watch Over Me

When he was old enough to enroll in public school, Julian remembers groups of Beatles fans lined up outside his school, waiting to see him. Inside the school things weren't much easier. Most of the students thought Julian was a "rich, snotty kid," and they treated him differently than they would have treated anyone else. And the bullies in his class picked on him because he had a famous father.

Yoko Ono, Julian, and John Lennon. After John divorced Cynthia and married Yoko, Julian saw his father infrequently. Here John had taken five-year-old Julian to the rehearsal of a television special featuring the Rolling Stones, another major singing group.

When life in London got to be too much for the Lennons, John moved his family outside of the city, and Julian was enrolled in the Kingsmeade school. It was at this school that Julian made his drawing of Lucy. It was also at Kingsmeade that he met Justin Clayton, a fellow student who shared an interest in music and who eventually became part of Julian Lennon's band.

Justin remembers that on the day Julian came to school, the headmistress made an announcement to the students. "We will be joined by the son of a pop star," she said. "Be nice to him."

Julian was five years old when his father and mother got divorced in 1968. Although John continued to see his son every other weekend, Julian and Cynthia Lennon were pretty much excluded from the Beatles and the activities that surrounded the group. John Lennon married Yoko Ono and became increasingly involved with musical projects with his new wife.

In 1970 Cynthia Lennon married Roberto Bassanini, and the couple opened a restaurant in London. But the marriage didn't last very long, and in 1974 Cynthia divorced Roberto and moved to North Wales.

By the end of 1971, when Julian was eight, John Lennon had moved to New York City with Yoko, leaving his firstborn son behind. Being separated by the Atlantic Ocean, Julian and his father rarely saw each other for a number of years. At school, Julian and his friend Justin were beginning to develop an interest in music, and together they took guitar lessons. The two boys had a keen interest in the early rock'n'roll songs such as "Roll Over Beethoven," "Kansas City," and "Rock Around the Clock."

Years later Julian and Justin would skip school to practice music, with Julian playing drums and Justin playing the guitar. Drums were the first musical instrument Julian ever played; he had picked up an interest in them after his father had given him a drum set as a present. Julian first started playing the piano seriously when he was thirteen years old.

Too Late for Goodbyes

During the summer of 1974, Julian was invited over to visit his father and Yoko at their New York apartment. At the time of Julian's visit, John Lennon was recording material for an album titled *Walls and Bridges*. While father and son were in a recording studio, John started playing the old rock song "Ya Ya" on the piano. Julian picked up a pair of drum sticks and tried to keep time on a snare drum.

What Julian didn't know was that John was taping the music. Later, John played the tape back to his son, and Julian heard himself playing for the first time.

At times, Julian's likeness to John is uncanny.

Julian had always adored his father, and being able to make music with him made a lasting impression on the eleven-year-old boy. He knew that some day he wanted to make music on his own.

The recording of the two Lennons playing around in the studio wound up as the final song on John's *Walls and Bridges*. The album credits for "Ya Ya" read: "Starring Julian Lennon on drums and Dad on piano and vocals."

"I loved it when we would sing and play together," Julian has said about those times with his father. "I felt really close to him."

John began inviting Julian for more frequent visits in 1977, and Julian, hungry for affection from his father, jumped at every opportunity. "I lived for birthdays and Christmas," Julian said, "just to be with him."

It was during this time that Sean, Julian's half-brother, was born. John, who had always felt guilty that he had not been a better father to Julian when he was small, was taking time out from his recording career to spend time with Sean.

In a number of ways, Julian felt like the forgotten son, particularly after Sean was born. Sean was always seen in photographs with John and Yoko, and a lot of John Lennon's *Double Fantasy* album which came out in 1980 contained songs about the joys of being a father to Sean.

To make matters worse for Julian, in 1978 Cynthia married John Twist, a man Julian never got along with too well. It is not surprising that Julian remembers being very unhappy while a teenager.

20

When Julian turned seventeen, his father threw a party for him aboard a boat in Florida, where John and Yoko were living for the spring months. That was the last time Julian ever saw his father; eight months later, on December 8, 1980, John Lennon was shot to death in New York City in front of the Dakota, the apartment building where he lived.

Two weeks before his death, John called Julian to play him two new songs that would be on the *Double Fantasy* album. Ironically, the songs were "I'm Losing You" and "Just Like Starting Over."

It was Julian's stepfather who told him that John had been murdered. Just at a time when it seemed that John and Julian were getting closer to one another, Julian's life was turned upside down.

Taking a Sad Song and Making It Better

There are many similarities in the lives of John and Julian Lennon. Even though their lives went down different roads, they experienced many of the same things. Both father and son suffered the pain of loss and separation during their lives.

When John Lennon was five years old, he too experienced the break-up of his family. His father, who had actually disappeared on a sea freighter years earlier, returned home unexpectedly to take John with him to New Zealand. His mother, Julia, however, would not

Julian at the piano on his 1985 concert tour.

hear of it, and took John with her to her sister Mimi's house in Liverpool.

Julia, meantime, had begun to enjoy the night life, and she, too, soon disappeared. For a few years Julia would show up unannounced to visit her son, demanding his love and affection. This time was very confusing for the boy.

This pattern, of course, is very similar to the way Julian grew up. His father, like John's, was absent a lot during this early childhood. Then at the age of five, Julian's parents divorced, and he seldom saw his father after that. Yet, the most profound parallel in the two Lennons' lives is how each lost a parent just at a time when they were getting reacquainted.

Like Julian, John had begun spending time with his absent parent during his teenage years. As the two got to know one another, John discovered he had a lot in common with his mother. She was spirited, and possessed the same kind of humor as John. But when John was eighteen, his mother was struck and killed by a car in front of his aunt Mimi's house. The death of John's mother was the ultimate abandonment that he never got over.

Artists have a rare ability that allows them to incorporate the events of their lives — good and bad — into their artwork. Painters often paint things that represent their feelings; songwriters are capable of the same things. The reason that some songs remain popular even twenty or thirty years after they were written is that the person who wrote the song managed to communicate certain feelings or emotions through the music and lyrics.

John Lennon wrote a lot about his feelings in such Beatles songs as "Help," "Norwegian Wood," "Julia," and others. Julian Lennon, on his first album, *Valotte*, took the sad moments of his life and tried to make them meaningful, not only to himself, but to anyone who listened to the record. One song is called "Too Late For Goodbyes," in which Julian writes about what it is like to have to say goodbye to someone one loves.

In the song called "Well I Don't Know," Julian voices some of the questions he has about his father's death.

Starting Over

After his father died, Julian Lennon went through a period of grieving and shock. He turned to music more and more often, trying to distance himself from the tragic event. Julian started jamming with musicians on the London club scene. He also began moving through the night life of London, showing up at the trendy clubs, fashion shows, and film premieres.

If Julian had felt as if he'd lived his life in the spotlight before, now it was even worse. The newspapers

Julian is now serious and confident about his music, whatever the instrument he expresses it in.

reported his every action and made it appear that all he ever did was get drunk. These reports were hardly true, and Julian had even said to his friends, "There are times when I wish I had been born Joe Average."

While making the rounds of London nightclubs, the

Julian's nineteenth birthday party, one of many occasions reported in the newspapers. As John's son, Julian was a good target for gossip in the press. Here Julian is talking to John Entwhistle of the group Who.

eighteen-year-old Julian met Dean Gordon, the man who would become the singer's manager. Dean saw a mixed-up and lonely person who was trying to have fun but wasn't managing to. Julian told people that he wanted to become a recording engineer, but this was probably because he didn't feel secure enough to tell people what he really wanted to do: write and record songs.

In his spare time, Julian was beginning to make cassette tapes of his music, but he never played the songs for his friends. One night, however, after Julian and Dean had been out at the clubs, Julian got up enough courage to play a tape. Dean thought it was a shame that Julian was not concentrating on his music, and began to encourage him to actively pursue his dreams.

With the encouragement from others, Julian began rehearsing with a band called Quasar. Julian's friend from school, Justin, also played with the group. Still, Julian wanted to wait a reasonable amount of time after his father's death to start a recording career. He didn't want people to think that he was trying to make it on his father's name and fame. By the time Julian was twenty, he realized that if he was serious about making music, he would have to try and get a recording contract.

The record companies, however, were not exactly eager to sign this celebrity's son who was busy getting his name in the paper for showing up at the London clubs. With Dean's help, Julian eventually signed with the British-based Charisma label after the company heard some of Julian's cassette tapes.

Late in 1983, Julian, Justin, and another guitar play-

Julian worked hard to make the music on *Valotte* the best he could. Long hours in the studio, rehearsing and recording, went into the album.

ing friend, Carlos Morales, left London for a French château called Valotte to practice and write the songs that would become the tracks for *Valotte*. Julian says that he went to the château not knowing what he was. When he left, he knew he was a musician.

Through his music, Julian wanted to sort out his feelings. While writing the lyrics for his album, Julian heeded the advice of his father. "Be simple and say what you want to say." By writing about things that were important to him, Julian Lennon took the first steps in assuming the responsibilities of growing up and becoming independent.

Even with all the rehearsals and support of his friends in his band, recording was a hard process for Julian. At first he was so shy that he would only sing in the studio when the lights were turned off so that no one could watch him. In the eight months it took to complete the album, however, Julian shed his shyness, and his true talents as a songwriter, singer, and musician blossomed.

Before he released his album, Julian visited Yoko Ono to play a tape of the music for her. After hearing the songs, she expressed her enthusiasm. Paul McCartney, who had always kept an eye on Julian, sent a telegram congratulating him on the good work.

Yesterday's Gone

When *Valotte* was released in 1984, it seemed that a shadow of John Lennon hung over the record. The voice that sang the songs sounded just like John Lennon's. Some people thought that the songs were old John Lennon songs that had just been released. Other people, those who knew that it was Julian Lennon, thought that the younger Lennon was deliberately trying to copy his father's reedy tenor singing style. For these reasons, and

Although Julian plays guitar, drums, and piano, sometimes onstage he just sings.

because of who Julian Lennon is, the public only listened to the record out of curiosity at first.

It was only natural that Julian's voice would sound a lot like his famous father's. "I can't help it," Julian has said, rightfully countering the criticism of his singing style. "I open my mouth, and that's what comes out. I'm not trying to copy anybody."

Soon, people started listening to Julian Lennon's music for its own charm, and the album sales started picking

The newly glamourous Julian dressed in a tuxedo to attend the Night of A Hundred Stars in New York.

up. In April of 1985, *Valotte* entered the Top Twenty on the American charts, and two songs — "Too Late for Goodbyes" and "Say You're Wrong" — began getting a lot of play on the radio stations.

Those close to Julian Lennon tell how recording *Valotte* helped Julian realize his personal worth and built his self-confidence. Although he is still shy, he is a witty man with a powerful imagination, and he likes to entertain his friends with jokes. Julian's naturally long, narrow face lost its droopy, sad look when he replaced his glasses with contact lenses.

His hair, which used to hang in his face, was cut to show off his sharp profile and the intense brown eyes he inherited from his father. An earring dangles from his left ear and spells out the Sanskrit letter of "om," which Julian picked simply because he liked the shape.

Seymou

The Dream Continues

On March 21, 1984, Yoko Ono dedicated Strawberry Fields, John Lennon's memorial garden in New York City's Central Park. Julian made a surprise visit to help out with the ceremonies, breaking the limited contact with Yoko and his half brother Sean. Because of his strong resemblance to John, Julian was afraid that his presence might bring back too many memories.

Although Julian was once jealous of Sean because of the attention given to him by John, the two half brothers

Julian on stage with his friend Justin Clayton, now a member of his band.

37

have actually been growing closer. Julian commented shortly after the dedication ceremonies that he hoped once Sean grew a little older the two could spend more time together.

In 1985, in San Antonio, Texas, Julian Lennon played on stage for the first time in his life. Along with a saxophone player, a bass guitarist and a drummer were Julian's two friends, Justin and Carlos. Although he plays the guitar, on stage Julian chose to play drums and keyboards.

The critics noticed how naturally Julian moved about the stage, as if he had been performing all of his life. And, for the first time in a long time, it looked as if Julian Lennon was having fun.

All across the United States, as Julian played, the crowds went crazy. Girls brought him flowers and other gifts, and everyone sang along with his songs. Although the reaction wasn't as feverish as the crowds that had met the Beatles twenty years earlier, history seemed to be repeating itself, and a new star was born.

Closing out his concerts, Julian played a three-song tribute to his late father. The first two songs were old rock'n'roll standards, "Stand by Me" and "Slippin' and Slidin'," both favorites of John Lennon that he had recorded in 1975 on the album *Rock'n'Roll*. The final number Julian performed was a Beatles song from 1965, "Day Tripper." Julian Lennon was returning the favor to his father for his lifetime of music.

At the end of his successful tour it was clear that Julian Lennon had decided that he could not deny his

Left to right, Sean Lennon, Yoko Ono, and Julian Lennon at the dedication of Strawberry Fields in New York, in memory of John Lennon.

past or the influence his father had on him. Just like other musicians before him, Julian Lennon was out to find himself through his music. Although his career has just begun, Julian Lennon's future looks bright.

Julian LENNON

D.L. Mabery

Julian Lennon is not just John Lennon's son.

As a member of the Beatles, John Lennon was one of the best-known rock stars in the 60s and 70s. Even after the Beatles broke up, he was a star, and his death shook millions.

Julian grew up surrounded by his father's publicity. He wanted to be a musician himself, but for years no one took him seriously— not even Julian.

Now Julian has had the courage to launch his own career. Everyone says he's like his father in both looks and voice. But no one can deny his talent is his own.

From a shy, awkward son, Julian has grown into a witty, sophisticated man on his own. This book tells his story.